THE WORLDS OF TSR

Random House and its affiliate companies have worldwide distribution rights in the book trade for English language products of TSR, Inc.

Distributed to the book and hobby trade in the United Kingdom by TSR Ltd.
Distributed to the toy and hobby trade by regional distributors.

First Printing: August 1994
Printed in the United States of America.
Library of Congress Catalog Card Number: 93-61476

9 8 7 6 5 4 3 2 1

ISBN: 1-56076-879-7

TSR, Inc.
P.O. Box 756
Lake Geneva, WI 53147
U.S.A.

TSR Ltd.
120 Church End, Cherry Hinton
Cambridge CB1 3LB
United Kingdom

JEFF EASLEY

QUESTION:
If a picture paints a thousand words, what creates a world?

ANSWER:
An artist, an image, and the beholder's imagination.

The creation of worlds

is TSR's stock in trade. Designers refine the research and theory, storytellers start the action from whence a new history can begin, and artists incorporate both into a visual model waiting to be animated by the involved observer. The TSR artists, past and present, are architects of the imagination, fleshing out visual landscapes of the fantastic from the ideas and descriptions of others. Medieval courts, gothic towers, barren deserts, and exotic cityscapes become as real as

JEFF EASLEY

photographs in the hands of such talented artists as Jeff Easley, Larry Elmore, and Clyde Caldwell.

Vampire counts, gladiators of the arena, wizened wizards, and jousting knights come to life on the canvases of Robh Ruppel, Brom, Fred Fields, Paul Jaquays, and Dana Knutson. Together with others too numerous to mention, they bring our worlds to life.

More than a tale to be listened to, or a script to be followed, the art of TSR takes you on a journey through such legendary worlds as Dragonlance, Greyhawk, Forgotten Realms, Ravenloft, and beyond.

Let them and their work be your tour guide through the landscapes of imagination that are

THE WORLDS OF TSR. . . .

WARNING:
HERE BE DRAGONS!

As you journey along the highroads and byways of the imagination, be ever watchful for what lurks around the corner. The favorite inhabitant of these worlds is of course that wonderful product of myth, imagination, and lore: the dragon.
Now dragons come in all sizes, shapes, and colors, with an equal variety of dispositions, personalities, and peccadillos. "Enemy," "ally," and "indifferent observer" are all possible monikers for the winged behemoth who might lurk around the next corner, over the next dale, or way overhead. . . . And up close is not the safest place to be when you discover that you haven't been invited "to lunch" but "as lunch."
Cartographers of the days of Christopher Columbus were "in the know" when dealing with the unknown, and their maps' labels would read, "Warning: Here be dragons!"

PROLOGUE

JEFF EASLEY

KEITH PARKINSON

CLYDE CALDWELL

JEFF EASLEY

JEFF EASLEY

BROM

FRED FIELDS

LARRY ELMORE

KEITH PARKINSON

DANILO GONZALES

BROM

LARRY ELMORE

CLYDE CALDWELL

CLYDE CALDWELL

KEITH PARKINSON

KEITH PARKINSON

JEFF EASLEY

JEFF EASLEY

LARRY ELMORE

It all starts so simply. A medieval countryside, a questing knight or bold adventurer, and a dragon. Dragons come in all shapes and sizes, their origins a mystery, their habits both varied and dangerous. Whether lurking around a mountaintop or in some dark cavern, they are more than willing to trade places with you and become the predator to your prey.

A dragon hunt is just one scene in an entire landscape of adventures. There are kingdoms to explore, chivalric royals to meet, princes and princesses to hobnob with, and courts that remind you of King Arthur and the days of yore. And of course every metaphoric Camelot has its metaphoric Merlin, a magician willing to share his secrets of magic and wonder . . . secrets that might be necessary for your continued survival in the land of adventure.

PART I
Landscapes of Adventure

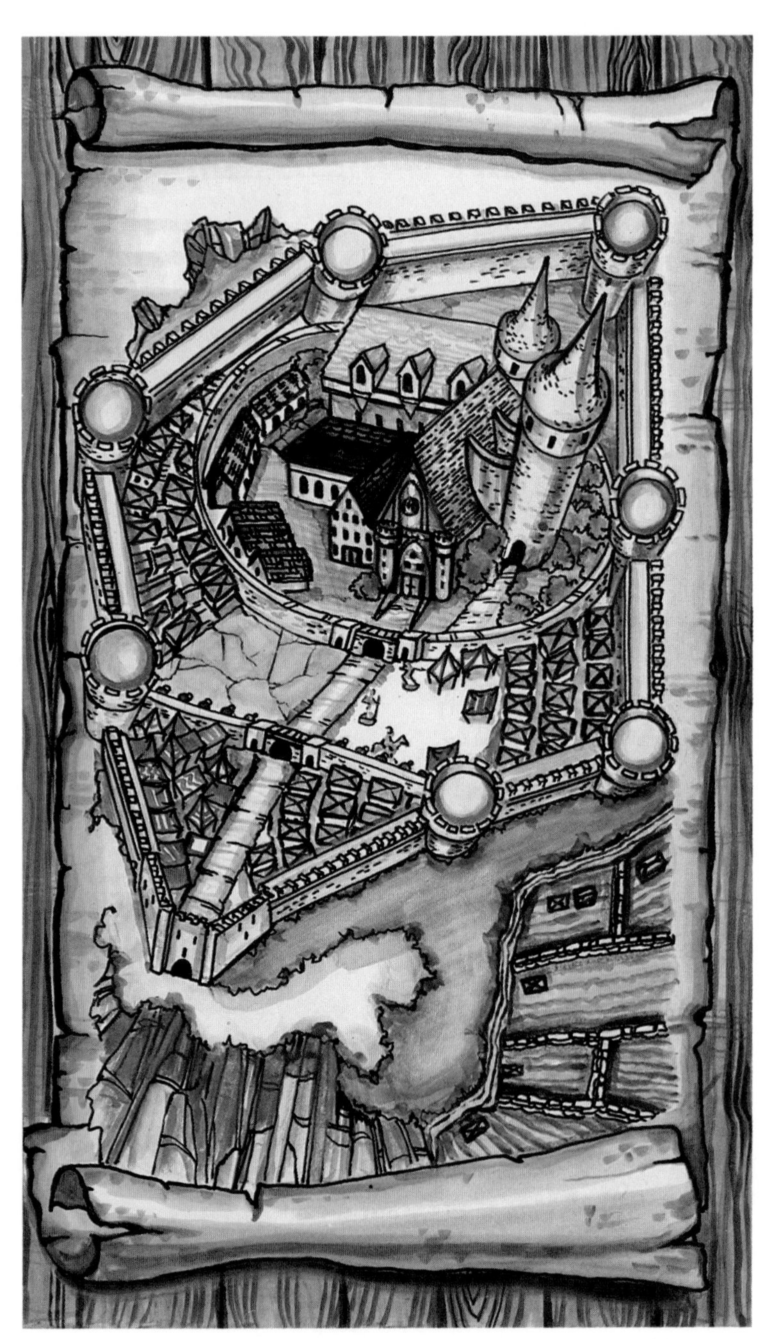

ROBIN RAAB

LARRY ELMORE

ROGER LOVELESS

JEFF EASLEY

ROBH RUPPEL

JEFF EASLEY

JEFF EASLEY

JEFF EASLEY

KEITH PARKINSON

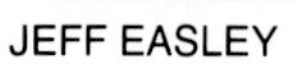

JEFF EASLEY

SAM RAKELAND

ROBH RUPPEL

ERIK OLSON

ERIK OLSON

ROGER LOVELESS

Not too far from the colorful
pageantry of courtly life are other
castles, dark castles filled with
treasures, secrets, and magic
items ripe for the picking.
You knock on the door, but it
looks as if nobody's home.
First you search high . . . but find
no treasure on the upper floors.
There is only one place left to go,
so you follow a cavernous
stairwell to the lower levels, down
to the dungeon.
Your way is illuminated solely by
the torch you carry. The dungeon
is cold and damp, and the echoes
of your footsteps play tricks
on your ears.
You are alone. The castle is
empty. The dungeon is deserted . . .
you hope.
Dungeons
are more
than just medieval
cellars occasionally used
for weapons storage and prisoner
confinement.

Advanced Dungeons & Dragons® 2nd Edition Game

PAUL JAQUAYS

JEFF EASLEY

Dungeons can be whole worlds unto themselves, stretching for miles underground, deeper and deeper into the bowels of the earth.

Traps have been set all around you.

Ogres, orcs, tigermen, or undead warriors might be lurking around the very next corner (not to mention the occasional evil wizard protecting his secrets or some subterranean dragon looking for his lunch).

You might think about turning back . . . but the treasure is sure to be right around the bend, and you did come here looking for adventure, right?

You step around the next corner to collect your booty . . . and a sudden breeze extinguishes your torch.

GLEN ORBIK

FRED FIELDS

The underground landscape of colorful adventure is replaced by pitch black, while you try to sort out the echoes of your footsteps from the other sounds you hear . . . and your imagination does the rest.

In terms of world building, the DUNGEONS & DRAGONS® game is where it all began.

A simple setting—an underground chamber filled with a winning combination of wonder and danger—started it all: dungeons, monsters, artifacts, weapons, jewels, dragons (of course), and any other element from beyond the limits of imagination.

Your options are determined by the characteristics of the role you play: a warrior brave and bold, a thief daring and stealthy, or a wizard secretive and powerful. Who you play is as unlimited as the field you play on, and that is limited only by your own sense of wonder and adventure.

The DUNGEONS & DRAGONS® and ADVANCED DUNGEONS & DRAGONS® games allow you to play in a landscape of imagination. You can set the course of history; gain experience, wealth, and knowledge; become a combination of Marco Polo, Conan, and Merlin; play individually or as part of a team. Dungeons, castles, cities, kingdoms, and even whole planets have been invented and detailed for your playing pleasure . . . and the art brings them to life, offering you an invitation to step inside and become part of the scenes of adventure.

FRED FIELDS

JEFF EASLEY

CAROL HEYER

JEFF EASLEY

FRED FIELDS

ERIK OLSON

KEITH PARKINSON

FRED FIELDS

FRED FIELDS

ROGER LOVELESS

JEFF EASLEY

JEFF EASLEY

The medieval world of make-believe is made more real through increased detail. Planets are given names like Oerth, Toril, and Krynn. Kingdoms and countries take on identities of their own. Personalities develop. Distinctions are made.

The landscape is no longer general. It is now precise. An ecology has developed.

A new world is born.

Adventures

The world of Greyhawk is located on the planet Oerth. It is the oldest of the ADVANCED DUNGEONS & DRAGONS® game worlds. The nameless dungeon of earlier adventures has become more advanced through locales such as the Temple of Elemental Evil, the Tomb of Horrors, and the City of Skulls. Memorable personalities such as Mordenkainen, Iuz the Evil, and Ivid the Undying come to life. A history develops. Events change the landscape. Politics get out of hand. Power-hungry forces vie for supremacy. War breaks out.

PART II
Landscapes of Wonder

CLYDE CALDWELL

GLEN ORBIK

The devastation of war is all around you. A civilization is being destroyed . . . but out of the ashes, a new one evolves. History continues for the planet Oerth, its landscape battered by war and the forces of evil.

JEFF EASLEY

The world evolves. The landscapes change.
Great cities fall to the ground.
Grand towers are besieged and crumble at the strain of oncoming enemy forces.
You are no longer facing only the monsters of the wild and traps laid to deter your greed.

JEFF EASLEY

PAUL JAQUAYS

ROGER RAUPP

CLYDE CALDWELL

KEITH PARKINSON

JEFF EASLEY

CLYDE CALDWELL

KEITH PARKINSON

PAUL JAQUAYS

A new terrain of adventure and wonder unfolds around you. The world of the Forgotten Realms is located on the planet Toril. Larger than the Greyhawk world in both geographic area and cultural diversity, the history of the Forgotten Realms evolves in a truly global sense.

Visit the frozen North and the Shining South.

Visit the Moonshaes and Evermeet, far off the Sword Coast.

See the wonders of Waterdeep, Cormyr, Phlan, Tantris, and Shadowdale, and meet their citizenry. Maybe the great Volo can be your guide.

Journey to the far reaches of the Hordelands or to the dinosaur-inhabited Jungles of Chult in search of adventure and excitement.

But more wonders exist below the surface.

Explore the ancient, secret treasure troves of Undermountain. Recover the remnants of the past as you tour the ruins of Zhentil Keep and Myth Drannor.

Sneak into the wondrous underground city of the Drow, Menzoberranzan, a sight not meant to be beheld by the eyes of mortal men.

Shake hands with Elminster, High Lady Alustriel, and Drizzt, the dark elf ranger.

Catch up on current events with King Azoun. See how the wars are faring.

No longer a Camelot wannabe, the world of the Forgotten Realms is much more real, a living landscape of opportunity.

ROBH RUPPEL

JOHN & LAURA LAKEY

ROBH RUPPEL

JEFF BUTLER

FRED FIELDS

VALERIE VALUSEK

JOHN & LAURA LAKEY

CLYDE CALDWELL

CLYDE CALDWELL

CLYDE CALDWELL

FRED FIELDS

FRED FIELDS

FRED FIELDS

FRED FIELDS

JEFF EASLEY

ROBH RUPPEL

JEFF EASLEY

JOHN & LAURA LAKEY

JOHN & LAURA LAKEY

FRED FIELDS

JEFF EASLEY

LARRY ELMORE

The world of Dragonlance is located on Krynn and is probably most famous for its legendary Cataclysm and War of the Lance, where the struggle between good and evil—the triumph of hope, honor, and camaraderie against overwhelming odds—is the subject of numerous tales and historical chronicles.

Krynn is a world of personalities: DRAGONLANCE® Saga

the good guys like Goldmoon, Tasslehoff, Caramon, and others; the bad guys like Toede, the

LARRY ELMORE

Dark Queen, and Ariakas;
the races like the kender, the dwarves, the minotaurs, and the dragons themselves.
Visit the past before the war, witness the signing of the Swordsheath Scroll, or attend a meeting of the legendary Knights of Solamnia.
Experience the Cataclysm.
Change the course of time.
Aid the Companions in their war to end all wars.
Become a witness to the history of Krynn . . . and beyond, as new legacies bear fruit and the world and its inhabitants continue to evolve.
The wonders never cease.

PAUL JAQUAYS

JEFF EASLEY

LARRY ELMORE

ELMORE 93

LARRY ELMORE

JEFF EASLEY

TIM HILDEBRANDT

TIM HILDEBRANDT

ROBH RUPPEL

BROM

BRUCE EAGLE

DAN FRAZIER

Welcome to the world of Mystara, our newest location with our oldest history.

Formerly the home of the DUNGEONS & DRAGONS® Game, Mystara has undergone a renovation, giving birth to a world that preserves the history of the old, energized with the freshness of the new.

Campaign

Chivalry . . . but not Camelot. Dragons . . . but not Krynn. New legends, new adventures, new landscapes . . . yet preserving the legacy of a land formerly called the Known World, complete with courts and pageantry, long-lost heirs, and intrigue.

The history is yours for the taking.

The picture that was worth a thousand words has become a gallery of history and alternatives. A simple courtly setting has become a living, breathing world, and an unnamed hero (or one-dimensional monster) has become a living, breathing character with a past and a future left at your disposal.

. . . and the wonders never cease.

DAN FRAZIER

GLEN ORBIK

PAUL JAQUAYS

PAUL JAQUAYS

PAUL JAQUAYS

ROBH RUPPEL

BROM

WALTER VELEZ

DAN FRAZIER

WALTER VELEZ

DAN FRAZIER

WALTER VELEZ

JOHN & LAURA LAKEY

Ravenloft

Gothic Adventures

Envision a world clouded in mystery. Visualize a graveyard where the dead no longer rest, an ill-equipped lab where a self-educated scientist harvests the remains of a patient as spare parts for his ill-made creation, or a deserted castle where long-dead former residents still roam the halls.

Imagine an island where spectral ships cruise the coastline, a crypt where liches and wraiths lie in wait for prey, or an isolated tower where an undead count romances his latest bride.

The world of Ravenloft encompasses all of these landscapes of dark mystery, and its denizens come from all walks (and crawls) of life.

PART III
Landscapes of Mystery, Darkness, and Light

ROBH RUPPEL

ROBH RUPPEL

ROGER LOVELESS

ROBH RUPPEL

Elegant vampires rule the night.
Werebeasts exult in their moonlight curse.
Undead creatures cling to the shadows, ashamed of their decaying flesh.
Menacing monks hold the secrets of your salvation . . . and damnation.
Shadows, fog, darkness, and mist shroud the landscape of mystery known as Ravenloft.

JEFF EASLEY

CLYDE CALDWELL

CLYDE CALDWELL

DANA KNUTSON

JEFF EASLEY

CLYDE CALDWELL

FRED FIELDS

CLYDE CALDWELL

CLYDE CALDWELL

JEFF EASLEY

DANA KNUTSON

CLYDE CALDWELL

ROBH RUPPEL

ROBH RUPPEL

ROBH RUPPEL

CLYDE CALDWELL

BROM

Envision a world of brutality where the spirit of free will is oppressed by the demands of survival, the darkness of evil, and the cruelty of greed and rage. Envision a barren landscape burnished by a dark sun, a landscape whose vitality has been drained by too many years of waste and corruption, a landscape where gladiatorial combat is an everyday occurrence, as well as an apt metaphor for the everyman's lot in life. Envision a world where all odds are against you.

Envision the world of Dark Sun. Now take everything you know about dwarves and dragons, elves and magic, and sorcerers and priests, and set it aside. On Athas, the fantasy landscape and all of its denizens have been changed.

BROM

BROM

BROM

Dragons are ancient, corrupt sorcerer-kings who long ago lost their humanity.

Dwarves are bold and broad warriors in the arena and in cities' back alleys.

. . . And magic is the power that has turned a once green and fertile world into a sun-scorched terrain of fire, dust, and dunes of desolation. A land where marauders roam free and sorcerous storms rage unhindered.

Hues of faded yellow, burnt umber and sepia, and fiery red color the landscape of darkness that is known as Dark Sun.

BROM

BROM

BROM

BROM

BROM

BROM

BROM

BROM

BROM

BROM

JEFF EASLEY

Envision a different sort of desert,
one full of life and light, basking
in the exoticism of the Middle East
and the Arabian Nights.

Al-Qadim®
Campaign

"Huzzah!
Huzzah!
Huzzah!
Visit the bazaar,"
the fakir's pitchman
calls.

Welcome to the Al-Qadim world
of Arabian adventures, the Land
of Fate, and the Cities of Delight,
Bone, and Assassins.

Welcome to our landscape of light
and enlightenment, where tales
from the past—of forty thieves
and a lamp, of ill-fated caravans
and long-lost kingdoms—abound.

FRED FIELDS

ROBH RUPPEL

JEFF EASLEY

Visit the seas of Golden Voyages, filled with pirates and dangers of the deep.
Visit the deserts, alive with secrets and treasures guarded by powerful djinn.
Assassins, sha'irs, yakmen, fakirs, and magicians are just some of the more colorful characters in the vast rainbow of color and light that make up the Arabian landscapes of Al-Qadim.

JEFF EASLEY

KARL WALLER

PHILLIP BABB

The mysteries of the undead,
color them blue and red.
The darkness of power,
burnt yellow, brown, and dour.
The rainbow of light,
the secrets and adventures
of the Arabian Night.
Ravenloft, Dark Sun, and Al-Qadim—
worlds of alternatives,
landscapes of variety.

CAROL HEYER

FRED FIELDS

HENRY MAYO

ROGER LOVELESS

CLYDE CALDWELL

FRED FIELDS

Not all of TSR's worlds have their origins in the fantasy of the past or legends. The future is also a fertile playing field for the imagination. Imagine a world of the far future, where society exists only through hints of our current culture, architecture, and civilization. It is a virtual no-man's land . . . which is not to say it is uninhabited. In the words of GAMMA WORLD® game creator James Ward, ". . . we took a planet much like Earth in the 23rd century, added a few terrible wars with radioactive fallout causing the usual nuclear winter, sprinkled in some bacterial warfare, and then had nature mutate everything in sight."

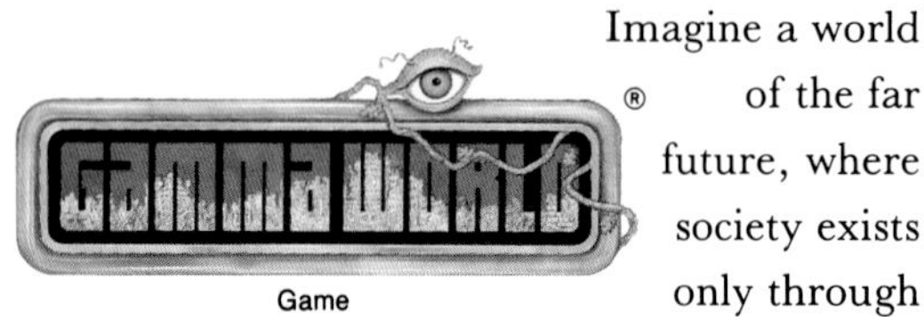

PART IV
Landscapes of Tomorrow and the Farthest Reaches of the Universe

KEITH PARKINSON

ERIK OLSON

Come see the sights!
Stand trial before a court of mutated zoo animals in a menagerie-based judge's chambers.
Fight the big, bad monsters while wearing your robot suit. Shoot that king-sized blaster.
Skim the surface of the desert with a ragtag troupe of rebels fleeing an all-powerful, not-quite-human warlord.
Have fun and adventure in a world gone crazy, where the heroes and heroines are as warped as the landscape.
The future can't possibly match the craziness of life in Gamma World.

BROM

FRED FIELDS

KEITH PARKINSON

FRED FIELDS

SAM RAKELAND

KEITH PARKINSON

CLYDE CALDWELL

LARRY ELMORE

JEFF EASLEY

BROM

KEITH PARKINSON

KEITH PARKINSON

Imagine a more traditional view
of the future.
A classic vision as old as pulp
science fiction itself.
You've been asleep for a very long
time, and during your rest the
world has changed.
No, you are not in the mutated
and whacked locales of
Gamma World.
You have journeyed back to the
golden age of science fiction.
Welcome to a
land of
space-skimmers,
skyscrapers, and
air pirates.

Cruise far above the urban
cityscape, rocket-belt on, blaster
in hand, Wilma by your side.
Welcome to the 25th century.
Welcome to the BUCK
ROGERS® XXVc™ and HIGH
ADVENTURE® game worlds,
where the future is filled with
adventure and good, clean fun.
From the 1920's to the 30's, to the
40's and beyond, the world of Buck
Rogers is meant for all seasons.

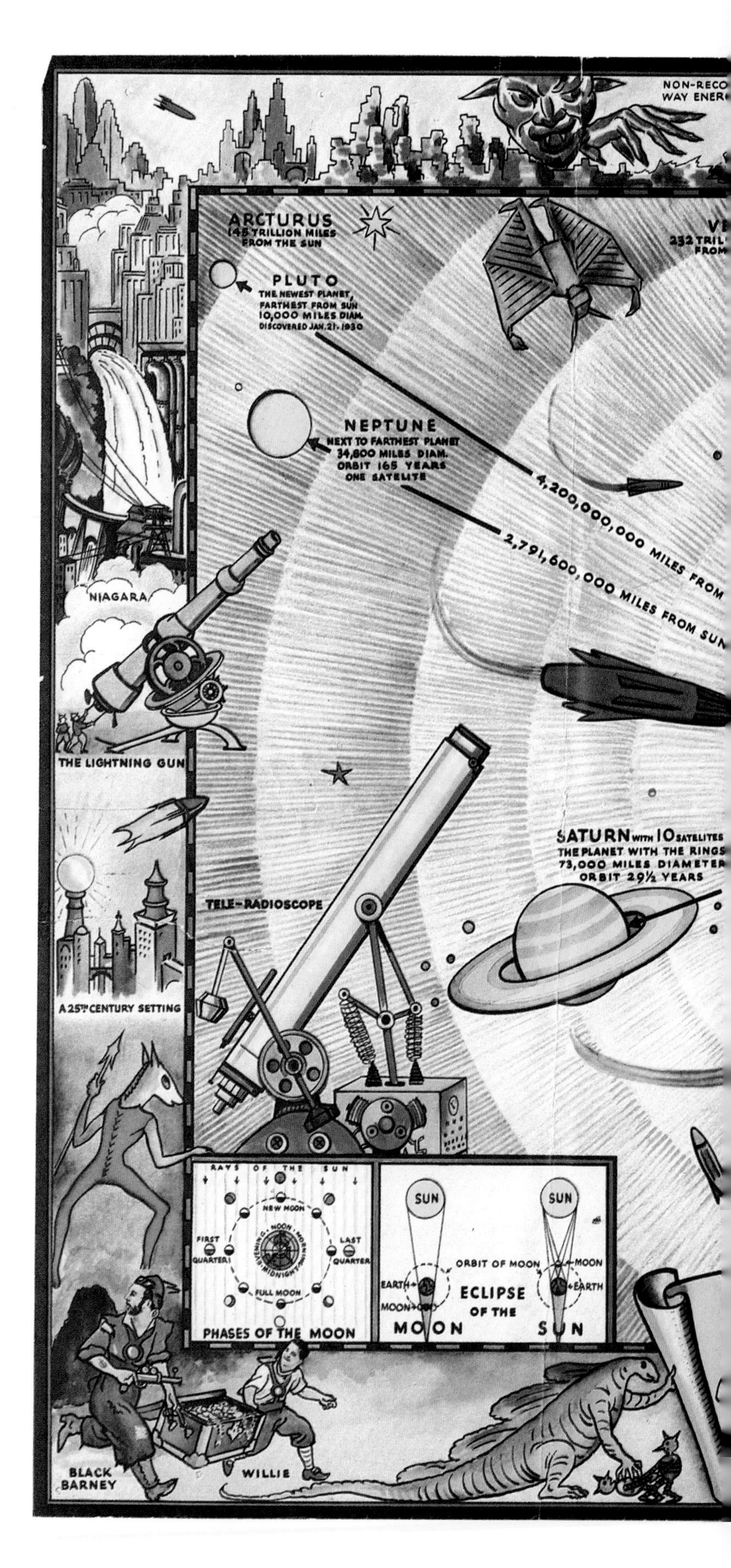

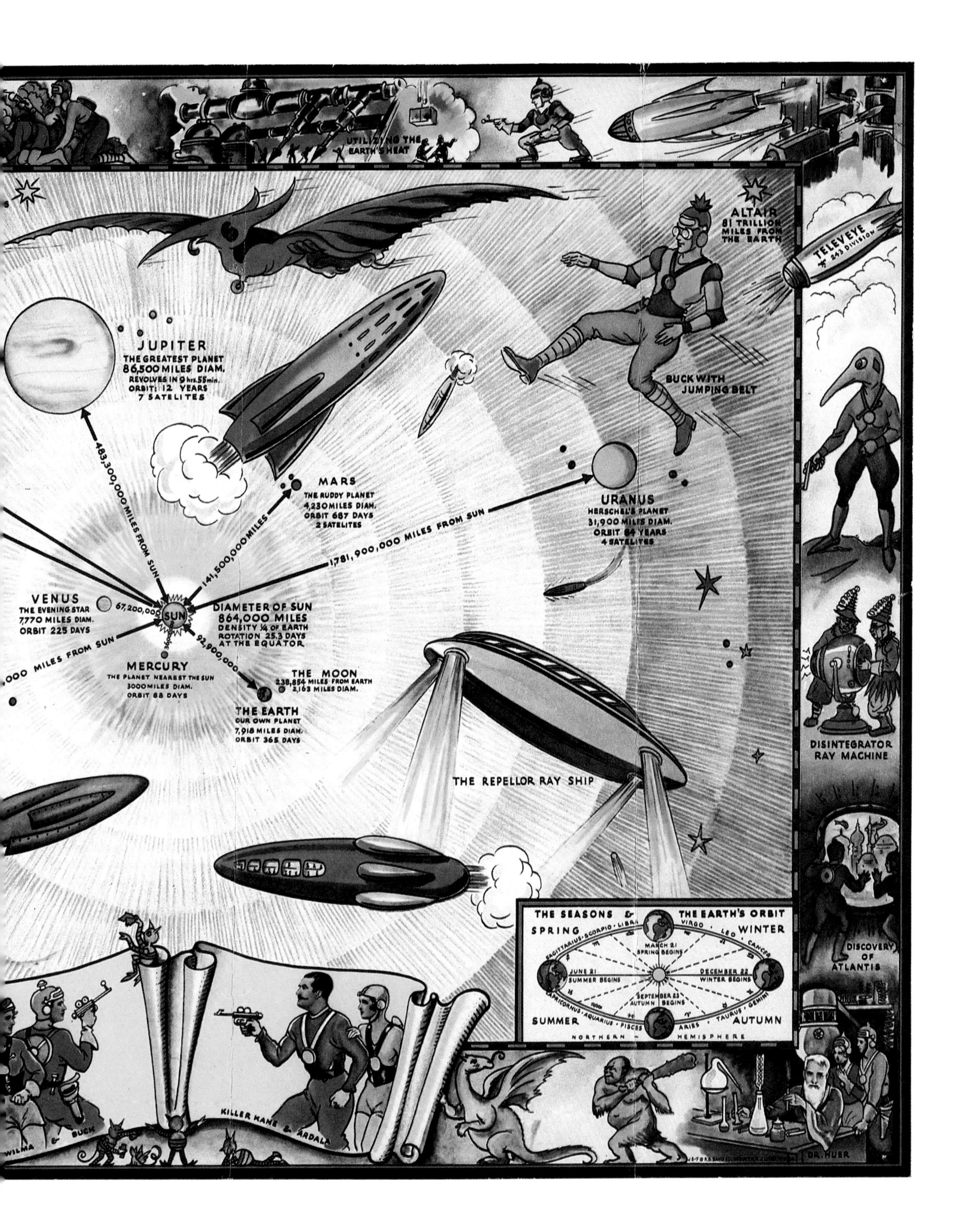

UTILIZING THE EARTH'S HEAT
ALTAIR
81 TRILLION MILES FROM THE EARTH
TELEVEYE
243 DIVISION
JUPITER
THE GREATEST PLANET
86,500 MILES DIAM.
REVOLVES IN 9 hrs. 55 min.
ORBIT: 12 YEARS
7 SATELITES
483,300,000 MILES FROM SUN
BUCK WITH JUMPING BELT
MARS
THE RUDDY PLANET
4,230 MILES DIAM.
ORBIT 687 DAYS
2 SATELITES
141,500,000 MILES
URANUS
HERSCHEL'S PLANET
31,900 MILES DIAM.
ORBIT 84 YEARS
4 SATELITES
1,781,900,000 MILES FROM SUN
VENUS
THE EVENING STAR
7,770 MILES DIAM.
ORBIT 225 DAYS
67,200,000
SUN
DIAMETER OF SUN
864,000 MILES
DENSITY ¼ OF EARTH
ROTATION 25.3 DAYS
AT THE EQUATOR
,000 MILES FROM SUN
92,900,000
MERCURY
THE PLANET NEAREST THE SUN
3000 MILES DIAM.
ORBIT 88 DAYS
THE MOON
238,854 MILES FROM EARTH
2,163 MILES DIAM.
THE EARTH
OUR OWN PLANET
7,918 MILES DIAM.
ORBIT 365 DAYS
DISINTEGRATOR RAY MACHINE
THE REPELLOR RAY SHIP
DISCOVERY OF ATLANTIS
THE SEASONS & THE EARTH'S ORBIT
SPRING
WINTER
SUMMER
AUTUMN
SAGITTARIUS · SCORPIO · LIBRA
VIRGO · LEO · CANCER
CAPRICORNUS · AQUARIUS · PISCES
ARIES · TAURUS · GEMINI
MARCH 21 SPRING BEGINS
JUNE 21 SUMMER BEGINS
DECEMBER 22 WINTER BEGINS
SEPTEMBER 23 AUTUMN BEGINS
NORTHERN — HEMISPHERE
WILMA & BUCK
KILLER KANE & ARDALA
DR. HUER

DEN BEAUVAIS

DEN BEAUVAIS

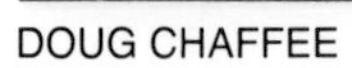
DOUG CHAFFEE

JEFF BUTLER

DAVID O. MILLER

JEFF BUTLER

JOHN & LAURA LAKEY

JEFF EASLEY

TOM BAXA

Imagine a different sort of
landscape.
Imagine a universe—existing
between worlds—that is magical
in nature rather than high tech.
This is not
the future,
nor is it
science fiction.
This is not outer space.
This is wildspace.

BROM

This is the SPELLJAMMER® game world, combining the celestial backdrops of space opera with the frigate-based nautical conflicts of the Barbary Coast, and set between the fantasy worlds upon whose terra firma we have adventured.
Sail by Krynn, Athas, Oerth, and Toril, seeing the worlds as only spacefarers can.
Set yourself behind the helm of a spelljammer, a dragonship, a squid, or a galleon. The choice is yours as you navigate your way through the far reaches of outer space along the ancient paths of the phlogiston.
Visit the Rock of Bral.
Meet the giff.
Travel through the Astromundi

ERIK OLSON

Cluster.
Stop by the worlds of DRAGONLANCE® and the FORGOTTEN REALMS® games while on your way to a martial campaign in the GREYHAWK® game world.

The choice is yours.
The scenery of the SPELLJAMMER® game setting spreads as far as the eye can see, and even farther than that by a universe or two as you travel beyond the moons and stars, across a cosmic landscape of legend and lore.
The wide open spaces of tomorrow and beyond are only limited by the confines of your imagination.

ERIK OLSON

DAVID O. MILLER

DAVID O. MILLER

PAUL JAQUAYS

JEFF EASLEY

KELLY FREAS

BROM

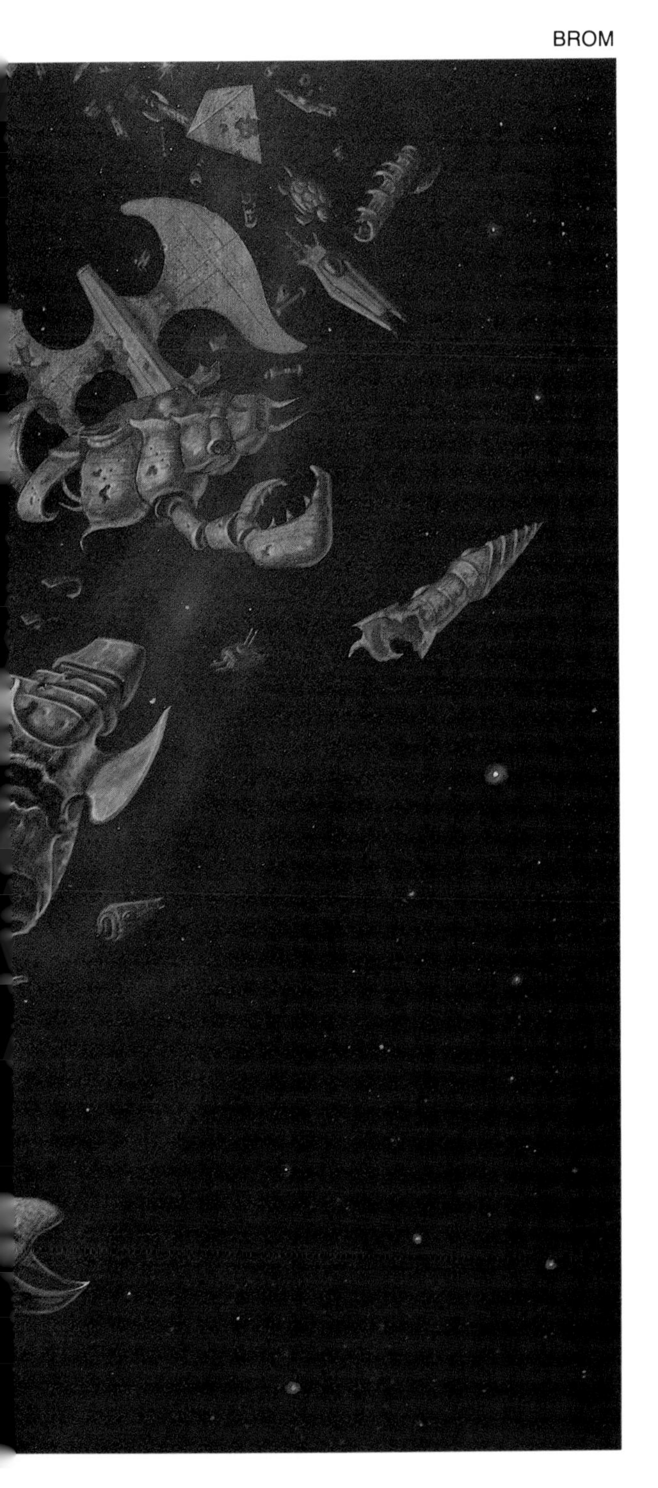

JIM HOLLOWAY

JIM HOLLOWAY

DAVID O. MILLER

JEFF EASLEY

KELLY FREAS

Realms of adventure.
Realms of wonder.
Realms of mystery, darkness, and light.
Realms of the future, and of space both outer and wild.
The choices are endless.
A thousand images, a thousand worlds, a thousand adventures

. . . and all of them are just the jumping-off point for TSR to lead you along the landscapes of imagination into a past that never was, a future that might still be, or just an alternative to day-to-day life.
Accept the invitation to take that first fantastic step . . .

. . . and beyond.

ROBH RUPPEL

JEFF EASLEY

Without the wondrous imaginations and skilled hands of the artists whose work is featured in this volume, publication of *The Worlds of TSR* would not have been possible. Also to be remembered are the many game designers, writers, and editors whose work laid the foundation for the creation of worlds.

Marlys Heeszel, Editor

ACKNOWLEDGMENTS

ART COORDINATION .... Peggy Cooper
ART DIRECTION .... Tom Lavely
DESIGN .... Dee Barnett
GRAPHIC SUPERVISION .... Sarah Feggestad
TEXT .... Brian M. Thomsen
TYPESETTING.......... Tracey Isler

BROM

INDEX TO ARTISTS' WORKS